10 Minute Shares

Simple Strategies for Making Money on the Share Market

Karen Newton

Publishing Details

This book is published by Karen Newton.   First Print: 2019

The right of Karen Newton to be identified as Author has been asserted in accordance with the Copyright, Designs and Patent Act 1988

Copyright © 2019 Karen Newton.

What people say about Karen Newton's training courses and books.

Connecting with Karen has changed my life. Karen has an accessible style, you can relate to her easily, she can captivate an audience and provides the steps which build a bridge for individuals to use in order to move from where they are now to where they want to be. Participating in the £2.73 Club has caused a paradigm shift in my own thinking about business and now a whole new future lays before me. Karen changes the lives of those ready to take action, she makes wealth accessible to everyone. **Marilyn Maidment – Director EquipYou Ltd**

*Karen's wealth of knowledge and experience gives an audience something to pay attention to and learn from. Karen is a generous, supportive and helpful lady whose willingness to help others through her £2.73 Club makes her someone you really should get to know.***Penny Jarman – Business Development Office at QualitySolicitors Rubin Lewis O'Brien**

Karen's wealth of knowledge and understanding of many businesses is interesting and inspiring. Overcoming adversity and representing women in non-traditional sectors resonates with our members. Thank you Karen for sharing your journey and showing a 'can do' attitude is everything! **Bethan Baldwin, Pride of Britain Fundraiser of the year 2015**

*I joined Karen's £2.73 mastermind last year and have learned so much about investing in her 4 categories. She says she can take you from zero to a million and she isn't kidding. Her mastermind group is a structured and proven formula that you can follow while also having the autonomy to explore new investments and ask her advice on these. I'm enjoying the learning and financial growth that being part of Karen's mastermind group provides.***Natasha Davies, Global Mindset Coach, Consultant and Author**

Fantastic book started reading it and couldn't put it down. Read the whole book in two days and ended up with bits of paper sticking out of the book at various points with pages I wanted to go back to. It's inspired me to make changes in my life. If you are looking to make a change in your financial future I highly recommend this book. **Peter**

Rowlands, P&M360 Photography, Storyteller Peter was talking about the book 'Surviving 2013' since reading the book he became a private coached client and is now a director of The £2.73 Club Limited

Been investing for years with no balance and over exposed in certain areas, now starting to finally get it, little steps and a lot of help and advice from Karen Newton I can begin to see the light at the end of the tunnel...**Michael Wheatle, Property Investor**

Just back from the Zero to Millionaire Seminar, What an amazing day, lots of great advice, tips and expertise, fantastic speakers and faultless knowledge, I am looking forward to putting into practice some of what I have learnt today. Thanks Again **Steve Gregory, MTS Ltd**

Karen is a great coach on how to build wealth through her £2.73 Club. Karen shows you a number of different strategies starting with very little money on how to build income and capital in a friendly supportive way. I have no hesitation in recommending Karen and her £2.73 Club if you want to learn how to build wealth. **Tony Thomas, Certified and Independent Financial Advisor**

Every time I meet Karen and/or attend one of her events I come away with more knowledge and understanding. Patient and supportive and oh so knowledgeable. Can't recommend highly enough.

Sarah Nightingale, ACT Training Ltd

Acknowledgments

There are many people who have helped and encouraged me either personally or through their books and videos on my journey to increasing my knowledge and wealth.

Brad Sugars of ActionCOACH was my first mentor. Through his training I learnt how to build business systems which have helped me grow several businesses throughout my working life. Finding that I had a knack for developing systems, I went on to study ISO9000 systems, using the skills to obtain certification for our NZ business. It became the first business in the Fire Protection Industry to achieve full certification for the whole business at a time when companies chose to certify only a part of their business.

In 1999, Robert Kiyosaki, the author of Rich Dad, Poor Dad ran a seminar in New Zealand where I was living at the time. I had the opportunity to spend some time with Robert after the event. His encouragement, additional books, videos and dvds became my bible to develop my own investment strategies.

Over the years I have developed my 4 Category Investment System of which share investing is an integral part. The other 3 categories are Property, Business and Bullion.

In New Zealand, I worked at Trust Bank NZ and spent a lot of time with managers who taught me about Fixed Cash Deposits, Share Investing and Forex Trading. On returning to the UK I met Ian Williams who trained me on Shares and Spread Trading through his course 'Trading the Easy Way'. I spent an intensive week of trading with Ian and he continued to mentor me for several years.

The next influences were Andrew Reynolds and Nick James. Both geniuses at Information Publishing. Through their training courses and seminars I developed my marketing skills to produce books, videos and seminars.

Following the 'Great Recession' of 2007 – 2014 the UK Government changed many rules and regulations about investment advice leaving many people, who were most in need of financial education, to fend for themselves. The £2.73 Club was started to provide financial education to these very people so they can make their own informed decisions and build their dream lifestyles and wealth. A big thank you to those people who tested the material which is now the basis of the training programmes we have developed over recent years and the clients who continue to build their wealth and lifestyles and prove our systems work.

One client, Peter Rowlands, became my business partner and co-director of the £2.73 Club. I could not have grown the business without his support and dedication.

Last but not least a huge thank you to my husband, Ron and daughter, Christina. They put up with me locked in an office writing or developing new systems and products. They support me through seminars and webinars. They help manage my investments while I do what I love the most – teach.

About the Author

My life seems to have naturally evolved around the world of finance first, on leaving school, working for Inland Revenue in the UK, then moving to New Zealand I went into Banking before setting up my own businesses and finally founding the £2.73 Club.

In 2000 a planned change of direction with investments saw my husband and I move from New Zealand to Australia but it was short lived. The death of my mother saw me return to the UK. Losing 6 members of my family in 8 months I stayed in the UK and looked at the opportunities around there. Borrowing £300 on a credit card, turning it into £10 million in just over 4 years, my dreams and journey of moving from employee to self-employed to business owner and finally investor was now a reality.

I started writing books about property investing in 2003. Today my books sell worldwide with my biggest markets being America, Canada, Australia and New Zealand. In 2014 I was awarded 'Entrepreneur of the Year' from America for my books. There are a wide range of books covering investment skills and strategies in Property, Business, Shares, Bullion and Personal Development.

In 2015, I started developing the £2.73 Club Investment System which involves 4 category investing. There are tens of thousands of investments but they can all be filtered into just 4 categories – Property, Business, Shares and Cash. The £2.73 Club teaches investment skills and strategies through modular learning. In May, 2016 the first clients tested the material for 6 months. By 2017 the £2.73 Club was teaching members how to start investing with little or no money. Today, we have 10 investment training groups and have started teaching our system in schools. More importantly, our training programs have helped several members become millionaires. Many clients become financially independent and helped our clients understand money for the first time. They now have the opportunity to create and live their dream lifestyles.

We run regular webinars and seminars and continue developing products and services for our clients.

The £2.73 Club was franchised in 2019 with our franchisees now running their own businesses teaching investment skills.

Personally, today, I have property investments in UK, France and Spain. A Share Investment Portfolio. Books that sell worldwide and an array of different businesses. I'm an Angel Investor with several businesses in the UK. In this capacity I providing not only funding but training on Business Planning and Quality Management Systems. Last but not least I am the founder and co-director of The £2.73 Club.

More Information visit:

www.karennewton.co.uk

www.facebook.com/273ClubLimited

Contents

The Goal

At the £2.73 Club we tell our members they need a goal.

It can be a simple goal of generating enough cash to go out for dinner. Going on that vacation they've been putting off for the past few years. Paying off some debt or buying the new house they've always wanted. It doesn't matter what the goal is as long as they and now you have something to aim for. Perhaps, start with a small goal or two and reward yourself as you get the results. It's something to prove to yourself this system works and the system does work if you put the time and effort into it.

Making money from investing is easy. You'll soon see how easy it is. But it doesn't matter how much money you can make if you don't have a goal to aim for then you aren't likely to be motivated to succeed. Ask yourself this question. What type of lifestyle, what dreams do you have that will ensure you get out of bed each morning eager to make some more money?

One client of the £2.73 Club suffers with severe depression. Depression that stopped her from working for months. She was self-employed and her business suffered when she had the bouts of depression. Not only did her business suffer but so did her income. She wanted to have sufficient income coming from her investments to ensure when or if she had another depression attack that there was enough money to support her and her family. On joining the Mastermind Training Group she set up an ISA Share Trading Account and invested in 2 rental properties. It took her 8 months to become financially free. Today, she has 5 rental properties with a target of buying 2 additional properties a year. An agent looks after the properties for her so she can sit back and let the income flow in.   She has a share portfolio that grows every month and can provide additional income if she needs it. In 2019, she took her first summer vacation with her family.

Another member wanted to pay off all her debts. Debts she had struggled with for several years. It took her just 9 months to become financially free.   Today, she has a successful coaching business and in the past year has taken several overseas holidays.

A third member wanted a specific and very expensive motorbike. It took him 14 months to make enough for his bike but he also made enough money to reduce his mortgage by half.

Each person had a specific goal in mind and achieved it. So, before you go any further in this book make a lifestyle goal and a financial goal. Have a reason to invest, something to motivate you and you will achieve it.

My Goal

My Goal is that you use the skills and knowledge provided in this book and the other books I have written, to build your wealth and dream lifestyle. If you need additional support then join our growing number of clients at the £2.73 Club and let us help you achieve your dreams.

ISA

In the UK we have a great tax-free product, which the government encourages you to use for your financial goals. It's called an ISA, and where possible we encourage you to take advantage of them.

If you are in a different country take a look at what your country offers to encourage you to invest in the most tax efficient way.

What is an ISA

An ISA is an Individual Savings Account that has tax saving benefits for investors. The best way to describe it is as a wrapper that goes around certain investments making them exempt from capital gains tax and income tax. The investment accounts are government approved schemes that comply with their rules and regulations. There are many types of ISA from saving for your first home, investing in Peer-2-Peer lending through approved platforms, cash ISA and Stocks & Shares ISA and these are just some of the different types available.

You can hold as many different types of ISA as you want as long as you are a resident of the UK. You can only hold one of each type of ISA. For example, you can't have two Stocks & Shares ISA's at the same time. You can, though, have one Stocks & Shares ISA and one Peer-2-Peep or any combination you choose.

You are provided with a maximum limit that can be paid into ISA each year. It is up to you how you invest the money. You can put everything into one ISA or you can split your allowance across all the ISA's you hold.

At the time of writing this book the annual allowance that can go into an ISA is £20,000. The limit is set each year by the Government. Although you are only allowed to deposit £20,000 per year into ISA there is no limit on how much you can make within your ISA.

There is a book by Guy Thomas – Free Capital: How 12 private investors made millions in their ISAs. It's an excellent book that takes you through different strategies each investor used to build more than a million in their ISAs at a time when limits on the amount you could invest were much lower than today. For many of the investors the limits at the time would have been around £1000 per year.

The book proves that with a strategy that suits you, you also can make a million or more in your ISA especially now you are allowed to deposit up to £20,000 a year. Later in this book, you will learn how compounding interest works and how you can build an enormous portfolio with just £100 deposited per month.

Why we use ISA

For buying shares use a Stocks & Shares ISA. As the aim of this book is to get you investing for yourself then the best Stocks & Shares ISA to use is a self-investing one. One that let's you buy and sell your own shares.

Using a Stocks & Shares ISA reduces the tax that is paid. You keep everything you make in dividends and in capital growth. There is no income tax and no capital gains tax to pay.

Sometimes tax is deducted from a dividend before you receive it in your account. Your online share broker will claim the tax back from Inland Revenue on your behalf and add it to your ISA.

An ISA allows you to gain maximum results from your investment by using tax benefits that are only available through your ISA account.

NOTE: ISA accounts are only available if you are resident in the UK. For other countries please check your country's tax or government sites for any similar accounts.

Pound Cost Averaging

Date	Share Price	Share Bought	Total Shares	Average Cost per Share
January	50p	200	200	50p
February	53p	188	388	51.5p
March	45p	222	610	0.49p
April	47p	212	822	0.48p
May dividend reinvested into shares £10	45p	22	844	0.47p
May	45p	222	1066	0.46p
June	45p	222	1288	0.46p
July	47p	212	1500	0.46p
August	45p	222	1722	0.46p
September	50p	200	1922	0.45p
October Dividend reinvested into shares £25	50p	50	1972	0.45p
October	47p	212	2184	0.45p
November	40p	250	2434	0.45p
December	42p	238	2672	0.44p

When buying and selling shares one of the skills used to manage profit/loss is known as Pound Cost Averaging (PCA).

What this means is that if you buy shares on a regular basis Pound Cost Averaging works out the average price a share owes you over a period of time and you can determine from that how much you need to sell a share for to make a profit or break even.

Share prices fluctuate on a daily, hourly or minute by minute basis. With PCA you buy a regular amount of shares in a company at the same time every month. The price will likely be higher or lower but you still buy your same amount of shares.

Example

In the example below £100 is used to buy shares in XYZ Company every month over a year. Dividends are only paid twice a year.

As you can see from the above chart, the share prices have fluctuated during the year from a high of 53p to a low of 40p. By staggering the purchases over a year and reinvesting the dividend the share owes the investor 44p. You are now in a position to sell the shares for 44p or a higher price and you will make a capital growth profit on the share.

How I Sold Laura Ashley for a Profit

Laura Ashley used to be one of my favourite companies to hold shares in. They regularly paid out dividends twice or three times a year ensuring anything from 12% - 18% yield per annum. However, they fell from my grace a few years ago.

At the time, I was purchasing Laura Ashley shares between the prices of 25p and 28p. I had quite a large holding in the company. When the company was sold to new owners the price dropped to 19p. Rather than panic because the price had dropped, I treated it as a sale and I bought a lot more shares at 19p, by doing this I dropped the average cost the shares owed me. The shares rallied up to 22p at which stage I sold my entire holdings in the company for a profit.

As I said earlier, share prices fluctuate on a second by second basis. Don't rely on your memory to determine how much that share owes you. Once you start buying and selling in lots of different companies you will not remember all the details. Use the work book to keep track. Remember you are working on facts not fiction.

If you are a company client then you will receive the workbook as part of your training on shares.

Benefits of Pound Cost Averaging (PCA)

PCA takes very little time or effort. Once you find a share to invest in it will take less than 10 minutes a month to monitor the performance of the share, invest your dividends and/or buy the next lot of shares.

PCA works best over 12 – 18 month period or longer. If you apply it over a shorter timeframe you don't get all the full benefits. The longer you maintain it the better the results.

PCA traditionally gives the investor an average 5% capital growth per year

If you invest in dividend income shares you will earn the percentage return on top of the capital growth.

Earn a dividend of £10 or more and companies like the Share Centre will auto invest the dividend into more shares at a fraction of the normal share trading price. As I write this if you use the Share Centre and hold Share plc 500 shares you get a discount off your trading costs. Normally, £7.50 you trade at £5.50. When using auto invest your reinvestment costs are in the pennies rather than pounds depending on the amount being reinvested.

Compound Effect

Before we go any further it's important to understand the compound effect.

Interest is the easiest way for me to describe the compounding effect although it can be applied to every aspect of your life helping you achieve amazing results. For example if you are overweight, you would go on a diet to lose the weight buy you don't just suddenly lose a stone. Week on week you lose a pound or two until over time you have lost a stone. That is called the Compounding Effect.

When I built my property portfolio I didn't go out and suddenly buy 60 properties. I bought 2 properties in year one. Year 2, I bought more and by year 4 I was buying one property a month. This is when the compounding effect was working well generating plenty of cash and allowing property to be bought more frequently.

Let's look at money and why we call ourselves the £2.73 Club.

Most people tell me they have no money to invest. Yet, if they saved £2.73 per day at the end of a year they will have saved £1000. The compounding effect in this instance is the repetition of saving £2.73 a day to have £1000. It is easier to find £2.73 per day than to come up with £1000 in one go.

You will be surprised at how much change you carry in your pocket or purse.

Compounding Interest

If you apply interest to the savings in a simple format it has an even greater effect. For the example below I have used 14% as the interest rate. I realise most people will say they can't get 14% it's too high. It's unrealistic. As investors with the £2.73 Club you will regularly be making high rates of returns. Property investments can bring in higher returns if you purchase the right type of properties (our investors are making 20% - 42%)

Different investments offer different yields for the calculations below we have taken the average our clients are obtaining across their portfolios as a base for the calculations.

With compounding interest you are reinvesting the interest you receive back into the investment. Earning interest on interest.

Compounding £2.73 per day with Interest

Year 1 saving £2.73 per day total saved is £1000 add interest at 14% total in savings is £1140. That's £1000 saved and £140 interest.

Year 2 continuing saving at £2.73 you have personally saved £2000. However, because you earned interest in the first year of £140 and reinvested it back into your account you have in savings is £2140. Add interest to the whole amount at 14% and the interest earned in the second year is £300. This is more than double the previous year as you are earning interest on interest. Your total savings are now £2440. The compounding effect is earning interest on interest together with your regular savings.

If you continue this process for 10 years you have personally saved a total of £10,000. Compound interest earned over the period is £12045 giving a total in savings of £22045. The figure is more than double what you personally saved.

At 20 years the effect is even greater still putting £2.73 a day into savings you have saved £20,000 but earning interest on interest, the compounding effect over the years makes your savings now worth £114,681. Over 20 years you have earned £94681 in interest. Equivalent to saving an additional £13.15 per day.

Now look at the effect at year 37. You have diligently kept putting £2.73 a day into savings. You have saved a total of £37,000. However, using the compounding effect with interest your pot of savings is now worth £1,130,221. The total interest you have earned is £1,093,221 which over the whole period is equivalent to saving an additional £80.95 per day.

The Compounding Effect has given you the equivalent of saving £83.68 per day (£80.95 and £2.73) for 37 years. But all you have been saving is £2.73 per day.

The more time you allow the compounding effect to work the better the results are for you.

Applying the compounding effect to shares

In New Zealand, a friend of my husband invested in shares. There was one company that each year offered him shares in lieu of a dividend. He accepted this as it saved him money on trading fees. The last time I spoke to him he had received just over 1 million shares as his dividend. Purely, from using the compounding effect. The shares were worth $3 each meaning his dividend was worth over $3 million. All he did was invest a certain amount each month into the same company and took shares in lieu of dividends until he decided he no longer needed to contribute to the holding from personal funds and he just let the dividend reinvest and grow.

Not so many companies in the UK offer shares in lieu of dividends. But places like the share centre offer an auto invest service for a few pennies instead of normal trading fees. You can still get the compounding effect working for you by auto investing.

Note: I mention the Share Centre as this is the platform I use for my shares. You can use any platform for share trading or investing. Check with your share platform if they offer autoinvest options.

I should mention here, that I am NOT affiliated in any way with the share centre nor do I receive and commissions. I use them because when dealing with small investment amounts they offer low trading costs incentives which helps you grow your portfolio quicker and easier.

Consistency over Time

Below is a chart that shows the compounding effect. In this example an initial investment of £2000 was used with £100 per month added. It takes about 15 years to become a millionaire.

The compounding effect is very low at the start but the longer you have the investment, the longer the compounding effect has to work and the greater the return becomes.

It takes consistency over time for the compounding effect to work.

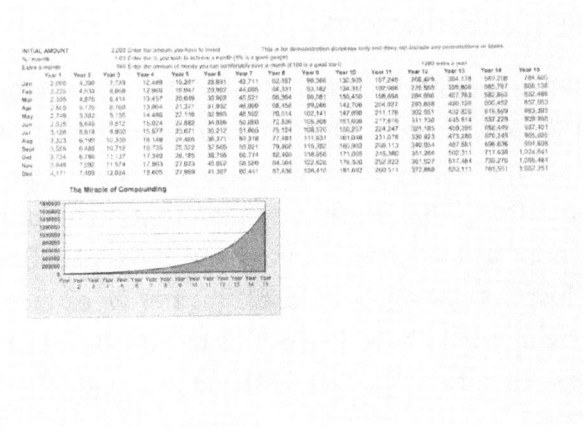

In the 2nd chart below the same example is used with a £3000 deposit and £100 per month over the same period of time. The time difference in achieving a £1 million in the account is only a few months.

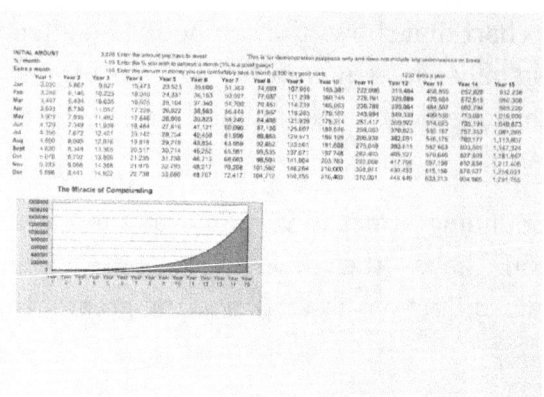

This shows that it doesn't matter where you start as long as you do start investing and give it sufficient time for the compounding effect to work.

If you can understand the concept of the compounding effect and apply it to various areas of your life you will be amazed at the results you can obtain through a small but consistent effort. You've already seen that if you put £2.73 a day in a jar at the end of a year you have £1000. If you want to lose weight and can lose 1 lbs per week at the end of a year you would have lost 52 lbs or equivalent of about 3.5 stones. What can you apply the compounding effect to in your life?

Dividend Investing

Dividend Investing is the third strategy we teach our clients together with Pound Cost Averaging and the Compounding Effect. These three strategies take less than 10 minutes a month and can be started with just £100 per month.

Terminology for Dividend Investing

Everything in life has its own language. If you talk to a car mechanic he will talk about plugs, injectors, ignition etc. If your car has a problem, being able to understand what the mechanic is talking about provides peace of mind that the mechanic understands the problem with the car and is capable of fixing it.

Investing is exactly the same. As we move through different investments there will be different languages (terminology) to learn. Here are a few that will help with share investing for dividends.

What is a Dividend?

First you need to understand what a share is. Simply it is part ownership in a company in exchange for any money you invest in it. In a private company, one that say you and I would own, there will be a few shares issued. My personal companies have 3 shares. I hold one, my husband holds one and our daughter holds one. At the end of the trading year we can decide to pay ourselves interest on the money we invested to start our company. This is called a dividend.

In a publicly listed company, (PLC) one that is listed on the share market, there are millions of shares issued in each company that we can buy and trade. During the year the company will state how much interest it intends to pay to each share. This is called a dividend.

How often is a dividend paid?

Each company will make a decision, depending on its profitability and cashflow, about how much dividend it will pay and how often it will pay it.

There are some companies that decide they can't afford to pay a dividend and prefer to build up the value in the company. Others will pay one, twice, three times, four times or 12 times a year.

As a dividend investor you are looking for higher frequency payers. As you start building your share portfolio you want shares that will be paying you on a monthly basis. This will help you generate income quicker, be able to buy more shares quicker, which in turn will grow the dividend you receive more quickly. It makes the compounding effect work faster.

Shares that pay monthly and quarterly provide the best flexibility to be able to grow your portfolio and allow the compound effect to kick in.

The best place to find the best monthly and quarterly payers is in the FTSE250 and FTSE350. Other indices are either too volatile or too risky to be able to monitor for just 10 minutes a month.

Volatility

To describe volatility think of the sea.

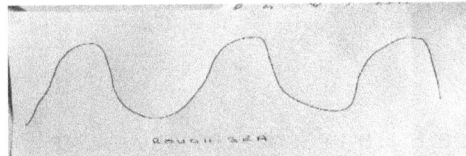

In a rough sea there are high peaks and low troughs. This represents the share price movement. FTSE100 shares are very volatile. The reason for this is pension schemes are legally bound to invest in FTSE100 companies. To make any money through buying and selling shares they will look for movement in price. They also manage millions of pounds. When they want to invest they will be looking for the lowest price possible to buy and the highest price possible to sell. Due to the amount of money they control if they buy shares at 5p less than normal price then the price falls. If they sell at 5p higher the share price goes up. This helps them manipulate price movement of the share so they can make money. Remember they are dealing with millions of pounds. When you have millions of pounds worth of shares a price of 1p or 2p makes a big difference in profit. This is why the FTSE 100 is so volatile.

When you first start investing in shares you don't want to be losing money due to volatility so avoid the FTSE100 shares until you have more knowledge and confidence to invest.

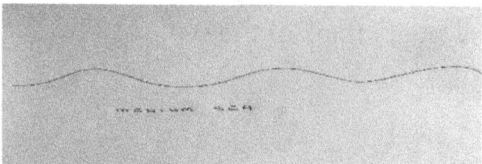

As you become more experienced as a share investor you are looking for shares which have a bit of movement so you can get capital growth. You don't want too much to start with as very volatile shares move too quickly for you to keep up with the movement unless you spend all day in front of a computer. You look for a medium sea wave that provides opportunities for growth but are still fairly stable.

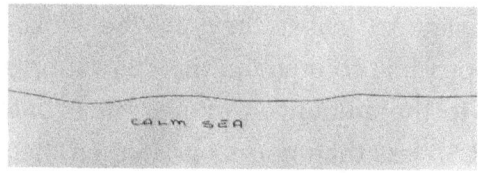

A calm sea has very slight movement in share price which is perfect for dividend investors. You are more interested in the value of the dividend rather than what the share price is doing. If the share price is fairly stable then the fear of losing the capital you invest into the share is lowered and you can concentrate more on making money from the dividends. FTSE250 and

350 shares tend to be more stable.

What is the FTSE?

The FTSE (Financial Times Stock Exchange) is an index that has a certain number of companies in it. Each day you will hear on the news that the FTSE (pronounced Footsee) is up or down. This represents the value of the companies listed in that index.

FTSE100 represents the top 100 companies in size and value listed on the exchange. FTSE250 represents the top 250 companies and so on.

There are other indices – FTSE Aim, FTSE Techmark, FTSE ORB and FTSE4 Good. Within each of those indices are more indices such as FTSE Aim50 and FTSE Techmark Mediscience etc.

Although you are using mainly FTSE250 and FTSE350 companies there are many Indices you can use once you become more experienced with shares.

The London Stock Exchange website or The Financial Times Newspaper provide information on many indices and companies which go way beyond the scope of this course.

Note: although this book is written for the British Market the strategies in here can be applied in any country

Ex-div

Ex-div or Ex-dividend is the last date that a share can transfer ownership and still qualify for the dividend. For example a company may have an ex-div date of 8th April and Paid date of 30th April. What that means is you need ownership of the share by 8th April to receive the dividend payout on the 30th April. If you get ownership on the 9th April then the person who owned the share on the 8th will be the one who receives the dividend.

It's worth remembering that buying the share and getting ownership of it don't happen on the same day. It might show up in your shares portfolio summary statement instantly you buy, but you don't get ownership until the transaction goes through your cash account. Therefore, I recommend when buying shares for dividend have around a week between purchase and ex-dividend date. Using the share example above you should purchase around the 1st April.

Paid

This is the date you can expect to receive the dividend in your cash account. Sometimes there may be a delay and payment goes in a day or two later. 99% of the time you will receive the dividend on the paid date.

Yield

This is the annualised interest rate based on the latest share price. If you were to put your money into a bank savings account they would tell you how much interest you would receive over the year, 0.05%, 1% etc. With shares the interest is calculated on how much dividend is received over the year and what the current share price is. If the yield shows at 10% and the share price goes up drastically the next day then yield would show as a reduced amount. If the share goes down in price then the yield will show as higher.

When checking the yield look at previous years to get an average of what the company has paid out overall in previous years.

Be cautious where you see very high interest returns. This may be a one off where the company has had some positive income, such as, sold off an asset and given the proceeds to shareholders in addition to normal share dividend or it could be the company is in trouble with share price dropping and returns seem to be high based on a below normal share price.

ISA Eligible

You are going to be using ISA's for trading. The reason for this is that as of 6th April 2017 you can invest up to £20,000 a year into an ISA account and not pay tax. You are going to be putting as much money as you can from your business into your ISA account along with anything else you can afford to add to the account. You, therefore, want to buy as many shares as you can within the ISA and earn income which is tax free.

EPS

Earnings per share. This is how much money the company is making based on the number of shares they have issued. It shows how well a company is doing. When looking at EPS if you see a negative figure (-4.5) it means the company lost wealth against the number of shares it has meaning it has less assets covering the value of the share. As a dividend investor you tend to look for companies that have around 7 as an EPS. That means they have 7 times more assets per share. Don't get fixated on 7 though nothing in shares is black and white. You operate in a grey area around which you have to make decisions. When starting to invest in shares just make sure the EPS is positive.

Monthly and Quarterly Dividends

When using a dividend investing strategy look for shares that pay their dividend on either monthly or quarterly.

In an example above I showed a share that goes ex-div on 1st April and pay the dividend on the 30th April. If a company has a yield of 6% and you receive the dividend on a monthly basis provided you reinvest the dividend every month the dividend yield is higher than 6%.

In the example below this is an actual company which pays a monthly dividend.

Company Information:

Yield 7.17%   Ex-div around 15th Monthly   Pays   dividend on last working day of the month

Dividend information pays a set amount of 0.50p per month with a bonus dividend paid once a year the previous annual amount being 1.06.

Share price hovers between 90p – 95p

For the example below I've assumed an initial Investment £2000 and dividends on auto invest. To make calculation easier we will assume consistent price of 90p to buy shares and no commissions.

Date	Shares Purchase with £2000	Total share holding	Dividend equivalent in shares	Value of Shares at 90p
January	2222	2222	12	£2010.60
February		2234	12	£2021.40
March		2246	12	2032.20
April		2258	12	2043.00
May		2270	12	2053.80
June		2282	13	2065.50
July		2295	13	2075.40
August		2306	13	2087.10
September		2319	13	2098.80
October		2332	42	2136.60
November		2374	13	2148.30
December		2387	13	2160.00

Investing £2000 at a yield rate of 7.17% would generate £143.40 interest total investment after 1 year equals £2143.40

By investing in monthly dividend shares at the same yield of 7.17% and compounding the amount monthly the interest earned is £160.00 this in effect equates to an annual yield of 8.00%

On the next page we'll look at an example of buying shares with a £3000 deposit with the same yield of 7.17% and see the difference in return possible with a higher deposit.

Date	Shares Bought with £3000	Total Share Holding	Dividend Equivalent in Share	Value of Shares at 90p
January	3333	3333	18	£3015.90
February		3351	18	£3032.10
March		3369	19	£3049.20
April		3388	19	£3066.30
May		3407	19	£3083.40
June		3426	19	£3100.50
July		3445	19	£3117.60
August		3464	19	£3134.70
September		3483	19	£3151.80
October		3502	62	£3207.60
November		3564	20	£3225.60
December		3584	20	£3243.60

The initial £1000 extra invested has generated more interest to the extent that by using the compounding effect the interest rate has been increased to 8.12%

Using the compounding effect with dividend investing

A little exercise for you. Work out what the Interest rate return is per year over 10 years. You'll be amazed at what the rate works out to. That is the power of the compounding effect.

Charting

A chart is one of the tools we look at to analyse the price and trend of a share.

To understand the concept of a tool think of your garden. You have a lawnmower, strimmer, hedge trimmer, loppers, rotary hoe, rake and the list goes on. Each tool has the ability to improve the overall appearance of your garden. However, each tool has a specific use. You understand the use of the tool and you improve your garden.

Most of the gardening equipment is bought as individual items. However, Ryobi came up with a system of buying one motor and clipping on the piece of equipment you want saving you considerable amounts of money buying a motor and attachments rather than 10 different pieces of equipment each with their own motor. So now with one motor you get different results improving your garden by changing the tool you are using. Strimmer for trimming edges of the lawn. Loppers will cut back any loose branches. Hedge Trimmer for tidying up the hedge.

Charting is similar. If you think of the chart as the motor. There are various items we can add to a chart to provide more information, each item (tool) produces a specific result which in turn helps us get a better picture and overall understanding about a particular share. But before we start looking at the tools we can apply to a chart let's look at the different types of charts available and how we would use them.

Below is a price summary chart for Laura Ashley. As you can see the chart is set to 1 year. This is the natural default when you use the Share Centre.

The chart clearly shows the share price has over a 12 month period been in a steady decline. When you see a share like this which is continually going down the natural instinct is to say this share is no good and forget about it but ....

Contrarian Investor

A Contrarian Investor is someone who would look at this share price and look for an opportunity to make money on the assumption the share price could go up. They would see the low prices and think 'sale' is there an opportunity to purchase low and sell high in the future.

However, just because the share is down in price you don't assume the price will go up. Instead you research the company, the market and use charts to analyse and try to predict where you think the share price will go.

In the case of the above chart and the history of Laura Ashley, as a dividend investor, I would not be buying any shares in this company. The continued downward trend of price and the lack of dividend would be of no interest when looking at this share price.

However, if I was looking at capital growth prospects, I would investigate this share and then put it in a watchlist until I was confident that if I bought it I could make some money. The above chart has different meaning for different types of strategies.

As a beginner for share investing, I recommend using the 3 strategies PCA, Dividend Investing and Compounding Effect.

Contrarian Investing for Growth

As a contrarian investor for Growth, there is a lot more investigation that is needed to analyse the future prospects of a company and if you think the company has the opportunity to increase it's share price.

In this actual example, I will demonstrate the type of investigation that I did to make some money from the ailing Corus Steel Company.

In the early 2000's I bought Corus shares for 2p a share and sold for just over £4.26 per share. There were several avenues of research I used to determine if the share had potential growth opportunities or not.

- Charts - I used Charts to look at the history of the share price. I also, used a comparison overlay against the FTSE100 to see how the share price was tracking against the index. I noted that all shares were down in value quite substantially so the share was tracking that price.

- The company was in financial difficulty and trying to restructure their business. Reading the reports and news articles it appeared that if certain things happened with their overseas companies and workers the prospect of staying in business was looking positive.
- The UK had been in a recession and was turning the economy around which indicated there was potential for share prices as a whole to go up.
- I researched other steel companies to see how they were performing around the world.
- I researched the manufacturing and building industries to look at potential contracts and where steel fitted into those marketing

All pieces of information that together built a picture of the company and helped me to decide yes, I would take the risk and buy the shares. I attempted to purchase shares at 1p per share but I was unable to purchase at that price. Eventually, my buy order was filled at 2p. The markets and economy improved, the share price went up and I sold at £4.26

This was a calculated risk because of the research I did into the company, the industry, the markets and the economy before buying. I had a checklist, my reasons for buying and I set about trying to prove my reasons wrong. When I was happy that it was a calculated risk that I could accept, I invested.

If you are intending to be a contrarian investor for growth, know there is much more risk involved than dividend investing and there are no short cuts to finding the information you need to be able to analyse the company, industry, markets and economy. It can take weeks or months of research. A 5 minutes research and buy attitude will 99% of the time lose you money.

Line Chart

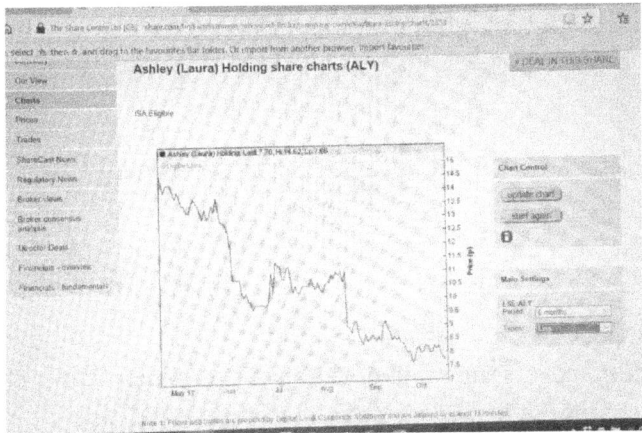

A Line Chart will provide a snapshot picture of the price of the share over a given period. The line chart is created using the closing day price for the share.

Sometime when analysing a share and overlaying information tools, it is easier to study the chart if it is a line chart.

Candlestick Chart

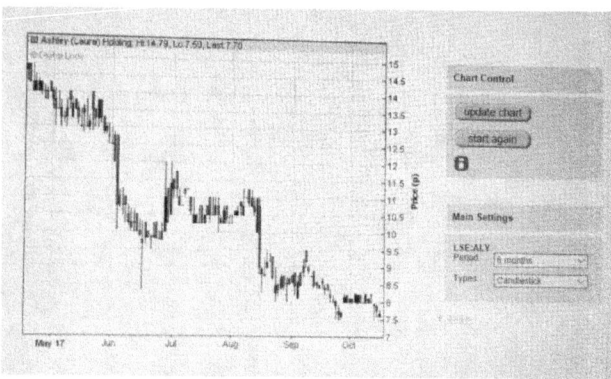

This picture covers the same price range over 6 months for Laura Ashley shares but in a Candlestick Chart format.

This chart shows us the range of movement in a share price throughout the day. Shares move in price every second of the day.

Buy and Sell is an agreement between two parties to the cost of a share which can vary from trade to trade. The Candlestick Chart will show you the highest price paid and the lowest price for the day.

The long thin black line (wick) indicates opening and closing prices. This is useful when the share is volatile or goes up or down suddenly. It gives you an overall picture of movement during the day and better understanding of the range of movement and direction the share is going.

This information is useful for a number of reasons.

1. If you use a stop loss strategy to protect your investment it will help with deciding where to place the stop loss. For instance if Laura Ashley has a trading range from 7p to 10p in one day. If you had set the stop loss at 7p then your shares would have sold at that price. You have no idea at what time of the day the 7p price came was hit. It could have been at 9:00am and then the share recovers to 10p during the day. It could be that the shares went up to 10p before dropping back to 7p. Either way if the shares have a stop loss of 7p they would have been sold. In this instance the stop loss could have been set at 6p and you would still be the owner of the share.

2. As we move into the next levels of investing and new strategies in share investment the movement in the share price determines when we buy or sell a share for profit.

3. There are alternative ways to invest in shares and use leverage to control more shares for less money. Share movement is critical to those strategies. Using and understanding Candlestick Charts is the difference between making money and going broke.

4. Candlestick charts can look very confusing when you first start using them. Persist with them and you will soon realise how much information can be gleamed very quickly by glancing at a candlestick chart.

Area Chart

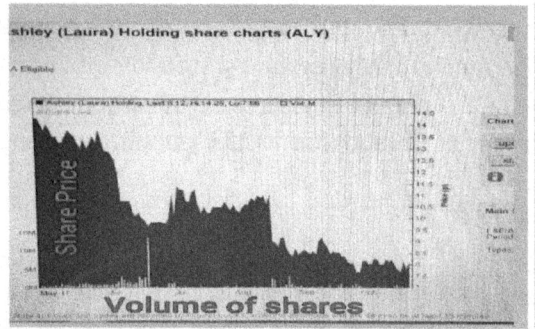

With the Area Chart we are again looking at Price Information presented in a different format as a Block Colour, in the example above its blue. However, across the bottom you can see little lines in different colours. The lines represent the volume of shares traded the colour changes for a buy or sell. Red means the share sold at lower than the stated price for the share at the time of the transaction. Blue means the share sold higher than the stated price for the share at the time of the transaction. Finally, grey or black shows the share sold for the stated price at the time. (Stated price is the price that is shown when you place your trade. For example the stated price might be 90p per share. Your platform broker will try to get the best deal possible for you and gets the shares at 89.8p – that trade will show as red because it's been bought slightly cheaper than the stated price)

Be careful when studying volume that you don't assume red and blue equates to shares going up or down. It is only a marker against the stated price at the time.

Volume is an indicator as to how active a share is. It gives you an indication as to what the market thinks about this share. For example, I know this share is normally fairly stable in volume of transactions and price. Then something happened to cause some spikes in activity. In the case of Laura Ashley the spike occurred when an unfavourable announcements were made that triggered a drop in price. Panic sellers were offloading their shares. The spikes coincide with a drop in price so we know its panic sellers. The colour also indicates high volume of sales.

*the unfavourable announcements for Laura Ashley were
- *change of ownership*
- *loss of contract with Homebase stores*
- *cut in dividend*
- *difficult trading climate*

Volume is important if you are going to trade in shares. By trading, I mean, buy and sell quickly to make a profit. As a trader you will need high trading volumes to ensure you can buy or sell quickly to make your profit. For example, if you buy a share with the expectation that the share will go up in value, having a low volume of trades means you could be waiting a long time for the share price to move. If you are waiting for the shares to go up and there is high volume trading you are more likely to get the price you want because high volume trading indicate big demand for the shares.

High Low Chart

This is different to a Candlestick chart in that the chart shows you the highs and lows of failed trades as well as completed trades.

For Instance, when you are buying or selling you have the option to accept a price or decline it. A declined price is still recorded in the HL chart. This chart is important because you can identify if there is support for a certain share price. This type of chart is used when using a support/resistance strategy for analysing share movement and probability of movement.

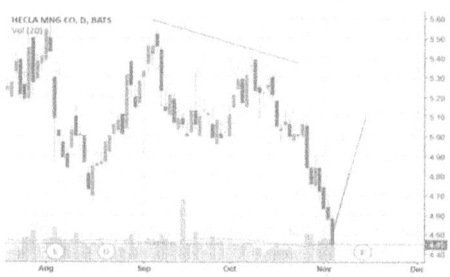

Open, High, Low, Close Chart (OHLC)

Open, High, Low, Close chart shows the movement within a day and indicates what the Opening and Closing price of the share was along with the Highs and Lows of the day. It shows if the closing price of the share is higher than the opening prices. This allows you to look for trends of an upward or downward movement. In the OHLC chart we look for upward T and an upside down ▯. The upward T shows that the share price opened and closed at the same position. Share movement was lower so the probability is that the share price will go up. With the upside down ▯ the share price opened and closed at the lower range of the share price which indicates a probability that the share price will go downwards.

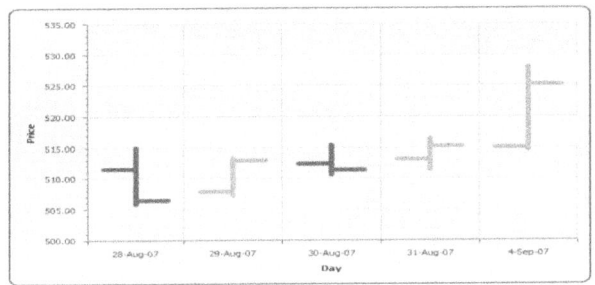

Logarithmic Chart

This chart shows the percentage movement of a share. For example if there was a share price movement of £5 and the share was originally valued at £10 it went up to £15 this would be equivalent to a 50% increase in the price movement of the share price. If the share was valued at £20 and went up to £25 this is equivalent of a 25% share increase.

Logarithmic charts are very handy if you are a trader. It's a way of looking for big movement/volatility in a share giving opportunities for traders to make some money.

Below are two charts for the same company over the same period.

Chart 1 is a logarithmic chart showing percentage movement

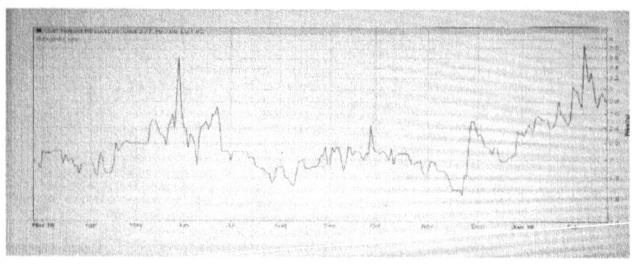

Chart 2 is a line chart showing the closing day price

Initially, you might be inclined to think they are the same chart. Upon closer inspection you can see the differences between percentage moves and closing day.

What Charts to Use When

As a dividend investor I use a few charts before making the decision to add a share to my Watch List. My chart preferences are

- Line Chart – which I use to look at the share price over a period of time. This gives a picture about share price movement. Is the company performing consistently or is it going down?

I also find it easier to use overlay tools on a line chart. The information is clearer for me. Having said that it is a personal choice as to which chart you use.

- Candlestick Chart – I use this one when I'm looking at price movement during the day. If I am looking to apply a "stop loss" the candlestick shows the lowest price sold during the day. I then have an indication of where I will be placing my stop loass

- OHLC Chart – this one provides open and close markers as well as price movement. It's a less cluttered chart then the Candlestick and I find easier to read. Again it comes down to preference. OHLC charts are not available on all platforms and on those platforms the Line Chart and Candlestick Charts will provide sufficient information for beginner investors.

Overlay Tools

As a dividend investor there are just a few overlay tools that we use for researching shares. These are Support, Resistance and Moving Averages. Over the next few pages we will look at examples of each type of tool.

Probability

The definition of probability is "the extent to which something is likely to happen". With share investing we use tools to determine what we think the probability of a share price moving up or down is. Moving Averages, Support and Resistance are tools which we use to help us draw a picture of the probability of the share price moving in a certain direction.

Nothing in share investing is black or white it is all about probability that something will happen.

Note: No matter how many tools we use we cannot predict for certain where a share price will go. We do not have all the information or a crystal ball to see what the markets are going to do. We do not know what is going to happen in the world that will affect the Share Markets. There could be a breakdown in Trade Agreements. Currently, there is a lot of volatility between America and China which impacts on the Markets. As an investor, we can only ever work on probability.

Moving Average

The moving average is a tool which works out the average price of a share over a given number of days. For example – is a share price for the past 20 days was static at £1 then the moving average for those 20 days would be £1.

However, we know that share prices tend to move a lot, each second of the day (see Candlestick Chart) so we use a tool that will calculate what the moving average is for a given period. Example – if we look at the 20 day moving average on the 21st March the software would calculate the average over the past 20 days ie from 1st March to 20th March. If we applied the 20 day moving average on the 31st March the calculation would be from 11th March to 30th March.

Moving average days can vary and you can set what period you want the calculation to be over.

In the following chart we are using a 20 day moving average (DMA)

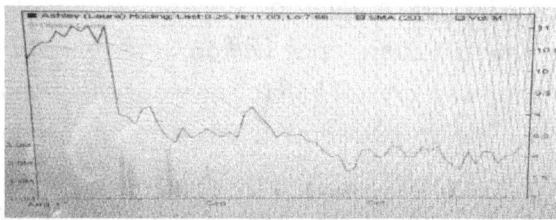

The chart above is a Line Chart (Blue Line) with an Overlayed 20 day Moving Average (Red Line) the coloured graph lines across the bottom indicate the volume of shares traded.

What we look for on a moving average is points where the moving average line crosses the Line Chart. This can be an indicator of future movements/direction the share price is likely to go. Remember we are looking at the probability of the share price moving in an upward or downward direction.

Looking at the above chart you can see in early August 17 the Moving Average Line crossed the Line Chart indicating the share price was likely to go upwards. Which it did before dropping down again. As you move across the chart you can see each time the line crosses the share went in a specific direction for a few days before changing direction again.

As a dividend investor, we are looking for shares that are more stable in price movement than this share which is in a downward trend. But there are different scenarios available with this share.

1. If you already hold shares in this company then the downward movement would help you buy more shares for your money and reduce the PCA on the shares.
2. If you are looking at a new investment and the other indicators are that this share could go up then you have the opportunity to purchase more shares for your money than you normally would.
3. You can look at the downward movement and place this share in your Watch List to keep monitoring.

4. Decide it is just too risky and move onto other shares to research.

Whatever, your strategy there is a opportunity with this share.

Watch List

Watch List is a tool that most share platforms offer that enables you to continue monitoring shares without the need to buy them. It saves time on researching shares from scratch each time you want to invest in new shares.

There is no time limit on how long shares can stay in your watch list. I've been known to hold shares for 2 – 3 years before thinking the time is right to invest in it.

Example – Pan African Resources is a share that was in my watch list for a couple of years. The shares were trading over £1 a share but when I researched them there was just something that said don't buy yet. A gut instinct. I put them in my watch list. Eventually the shares dropped in price right down to around 7p per share and then started going back up again. I bought them at 8p a share and as I write this they are trading at 10.68p a share. Imagine how much money I could have lost if I had bought at £1 per share. By being patient and waiting for the trade to come my way I have made a profit rather than lost money.

Debenhams was an example of a company that sat for 3 years in my watchlist. I didn't buy and with their demise this year they have now been removed from the watchlist.

Put everything into a watch list before you buy and monitor the shares. When you think the price is right buy them. If you never get the right price just keep monitoring until you do or decide to remove them from the watch list. Rush into investing and you'll lose money. Be patient, do your research, wait for the deal to come your way.

An old coach of mine used to say there are one in a million deal every day. Be patient and wait till the right one comes along. That advice applies to every investment not just shares.

Resistance & Support Indicators (RSI)

Support

Imagine jumping up and down on the floor. You expect the floor to "support" your weight. Support for shares is similar. You are looking at the lower percentage of the share and looking to see if there is support for the share price to stop at it's lowest point or will it go lower.

Resistance

Think of resistance as a ceiling. When you are jumping can you break through the ceiling or does it stop you from moving upwards?

Shares have imaginery boundaries which are based on the perception of value of a share. If a share price was £1 and another company had a share price of £1000 you would image that the thousand pound share company was more valuable than the one pound share company. It's a bit like the difference between Harrods of London and your local corner store.

The perception is the £1 share is based on the value of the company. If the shares suddenly leapt to £100 you would expect the company to improve in value. But for the share to get up to £100 per share there are lots of imaginery ceilings it needs to break. This is known as resistance.

As an investor you are looking for evidence that the share can break through the imaginery ceiling and stay up there.

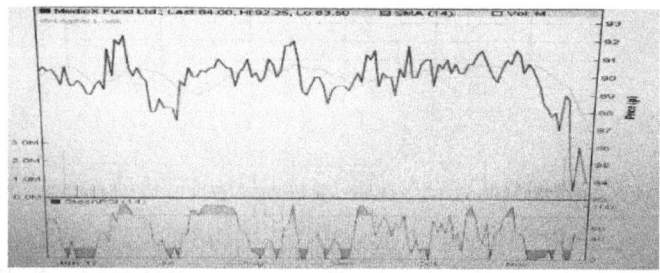

In the above line chart we have a 14 day moving average and below the chart a 14 day Resistance and Support (RSI) Indicator. So what are we looking for?

The Moving Average line does not have a current cross-over so the share price looks likely to continue going down or will it? This is where we start using the RSI.

Resistance – which is the red block colour on the lower chart shows the price has gone up but there is no support for it stay up in price. You can see the price dropped back down and there are solid blue blocks indicating it has stayed down for a while.

Support – which is the blue block colour across the bottom of the lower chart shows the price keeps going up but comes back down again. Take a close look at the last trading day on the graph. The share looks like it was coming out of the "support" section and could be turning upwards again. But the last day shows closing price heading down again.

As an exercise – make a decision now based on the chart information above. Would you buy the share or would you wait?

Now you've made a decision, look the chart up and see what happened to the price.

Fundamental Analysis

Fundamental Analysis is looking at a specific investment today with the information available today and making a decision, today based on that information.

For example – If I went to buy a property and the roof leaked, every room needed redecorating, it needed a new kitchen and it new bathroom, yet, once all the work was done the property would have a value of £100,000. If I decide to buy it I wouldn't be paying £100,000 because the house isn't currently worth that and I might buy it for £70,000.

This is fundamental analysis. Looking at the current information available and determining if it is worth buying today.

The emphasis is on TODAY.

When you first start investing in shares you use Fundamental Analysis to look at the current situation of the share and see if you think that share is worth buying based on today's information.

You have seen the tools to us which are Charts, Moving Averages, Support and Resistance Indicators. This provides you with all the current information you need to make a decision to buy or not.

If's don't work

For fundamental analysis you are looking at the "now". You may be thinking if this happens then the market will do this and the share price will go to that. If, is gambling and wishful thinking. You are analysising the "now". Get that wrong and you will lose money.

Dividend Investing

If you are investing for dividend then you will look at the dividend yield and frequency of payment together with Charts, Moving Averages, Support and Resistance Indicators. These are all the tools that you need to start a dividend investing portfolio.

You will now be able to build a portfolio of shares using PCA and Compounding Effect that can be very lucrative to you as an investor over time.

Mixed Strategies

Throughout this book we have talked about using 3 strategies – Dividend Investing, PCA and Compounding Effect. Dividend Investing is the key strategy. You are buying shares for dividend.

As I mentioned earlier there are different strategies you can use. Dividend Investing is the best strategy for beginners as it provides a more stable, confidence building, long term strategy. Adding the PCA strategy helps to even out the ups and downs of the market, give some capital growth and provide a dividend income. When prices go down you can buy more shares and increase the amount you receive in dividend income.

If you bought shares for a growth strategy, you would be protecting your capital and in that instance your analysis is different as is your reaction to a downward price movement. You would be selling shares rather than buying more.

If you have bought shares for dividend stick with dividend strategies. If you have shares for growth stick with that strategy. Mixing strategies will only ensure you miss out on dividends and capital.

10 Minute Shares

There's no getting around it, I like simplicity and I'm a lazy investor. By that I mean I don't like watching a screen all day waiting to see if my shares are going up a penny or two to make a profit. Although, I do trade when the market suits trading I much prefer slow and steady, less monitoring dividend investing. This takes me about 10 minutes a month and provides excellent results over time.

Below is my strategy for 10 Minute Share Investing.

Investing for Dividend

I have a standing order which pays into my share account.

Monthly Dividend Shares

- Reinvest the dividends each month on auto invest
- Purchase new shares each month in the same companies

Quarterly Dividend Shares

- Reinvest the dividends each month on auto invest
- Purchase new shares each month in the quarterly share which is about to go ex-dividend ready for the next dividend payout

That whole process takes about 2 minutes after which I look at the shares in my watch list to see if anything looks interesting to buy. Any remaining time is spent researching new shares to add to the watch list. Dull, boring, lazy investing which proves lucrative month after month.

That's it

It's a simple strategy that takes around 10 minutes per month, produces a good dividend yield and sees my portfolio continue to grow. I just patiently sit back and let the compounding effect work it's magic and build my wealth.

That's 10 Minute Shares.

Additional Resources

Criteria Checklist

I have created a criteria for each share I invest in depending on the strategy I am using. There are so many shares that unless you have a computer mind or a Warren Buffett mind you will not remember the shares you are looking at. I fill in a sheet for each share and keep them in a folder with comments to jog my memory on the strategy I was researching for the share.

It doesn't need to be complicated just something to reduce the amount of research you do in the future.

Members of our training groups will have a sample Criteria Checklist in the Wealth Monitoring Cashflow Workbooks

Share Portfolio Workbook

The Share Portfolio Workbook is a monitoring tool for working out what price the share owes you. When you use a PCA strategy you are buying at different prices. This workbook calculates the average price owed to you per share helping you to set sell prices for profit. If you are dividend investing it will take into account the dividend in the calculation

Members of our training groups receive this workbook free with Year 1 module 4 training materials.

Podcasts & Webinars

Podcasts and Webinars are available free of charge from https://club273.podbean.com

And our Youtube Channel 273 Club.

Newsletter

There is a free monthly newsletter you can subscribe to. The newsletter covers all aspects of investing including shares. Just message us at www.facebook.com/273clublimited with your email address to be added to the list

Other Books by the Author

We use 4 category investing – Property, Shares, Business and Cash. Network Marketers already generate the cash but don't know where to invest their money.

This books is for anyone who already has a Network Marketing Business or any type of business which is generating income. It shows how business fits into our investment strategies and how to find the best investments with your surplus cash to provide a balanced investment portfolio.

This book is available through Amazon/Kindle as paperback and ebook.

Niche Marketing is also known as Information Products and Internet Marketing. It's about finding a Niche of clients who are interested in a specific topic and creating products to meet the clients needs. The products can be books, videos, podcasts, webinars and seminars etc. that provide the client with the additional information they require.

The book is available through Amazon/Kindle as a paperback and ebook.

Surviving 2013 was part of a series of books which dealt with investment strategies during the great recession from 2008-2014

The book is still a good overall investment book with plenty of ways to invest to protect your assets and income during a downturn market.

Karen Newton is the Author of 16 books on Financial Education and Personal Development. Books which remain in print are available through Amazon as Paperbacks, ebooks or through the Kindle Library.

£2.73 Club
FROM ZERO TO MILLIONAIRE
Wealth Training

The £2.73 Club teaches you how to build the wealth so you can live your dream lifestyle. The focus is set your Lifestyle Goals and as you create your wealth use it to build the lifestyle you want.

The £2.73 Club is an investment training club teaching investment skills through modular learning, webinars, seminars podcasts and videos. We advocate you can start with zero, generating income as you progress. Most of our clients can generate around £50 - £100 in their first month easily covering their monthly members fee.

The £2.73 Club is unique in that most wealth coaching companies focus on just one category of investing we teach 4 cateogry investing – Property, Business, Shares and Bullion. The reason we teach 4 catergories is the belief that during volatile economic times usually one category will perform well. Sometimes 2 categories will do well while other perform badly. We believe that by investing in all 4 categories you ensure you always have investments performing well providing additional security to investors.

For more information about the £2.73 Club we can be found at www.facebook.com/273clublimited

The £2.73 Club Structure

We offer a variety of ways to learn within the £2.73 Club.

Mastermind Groups – these are our main training groups. Our clients meet monthly for about 2 hours where they work through a module and discuss their progress from the previous month. They use a workbook to record their progress and monitor their wealth creation. They are small groups with around 10 people per group. Details can be found on our facebook page for the next group.

Online Groups – We recognise that not everyone can attend our training groups so we offer an online alternative. These are larger groups but still have access to the same modular information together with a Facebook Live session which is recorded and available in your group to view at any time.

Webinars – these are free webinars covering a variety of topics they last for about 30 minutes. The property webinar is held on the 2nd and 4th Tuesday monthly with a video of the webinar available on our YouTube channel. Details of up and coming webinars are available in the events section of our Facebook page.

Seminars – a variety of seminars are held each month details of which can be found on our facebook page or on eventbrite. Our popular From Zero to Millionaire Webinar is the starter for the Mastermind Groups and is held usually held just prior to a new Mastermind Group starting. Other seminars include Property; Lease Options; Shares Investing and Desktop Publishing. Again, check the Events section of our Facebook page or Eventbrite for details.

Podcasts – are available at https://club273.podbean.com

Youtube videos – can be found on youtube at 273 Club

Franchise Opportunities

Financial investing skills and knowledge can be used in almost any country, as most countries operate similar financial systems.

The £2.73 Club is franchised with licences/agreements being available worldwide.

If you are interested in a franchise please contact us via our facebook page www.facebook.com/273ClubLimited

www.ingramcontent.com/pod-product-compliance
Lightning Source LLC
Chambersburg PA
CBHW070439180526
45158CB00019B/1767